If ever the animal kingdom was aware of its dangers

Resulting from careless actions of strangers

Poaching, natural disaster, and climate change

Pollution, disease, and shrunken habitat range

Ruination at the creatures' expense

Carefree, forgotten, and without defense.

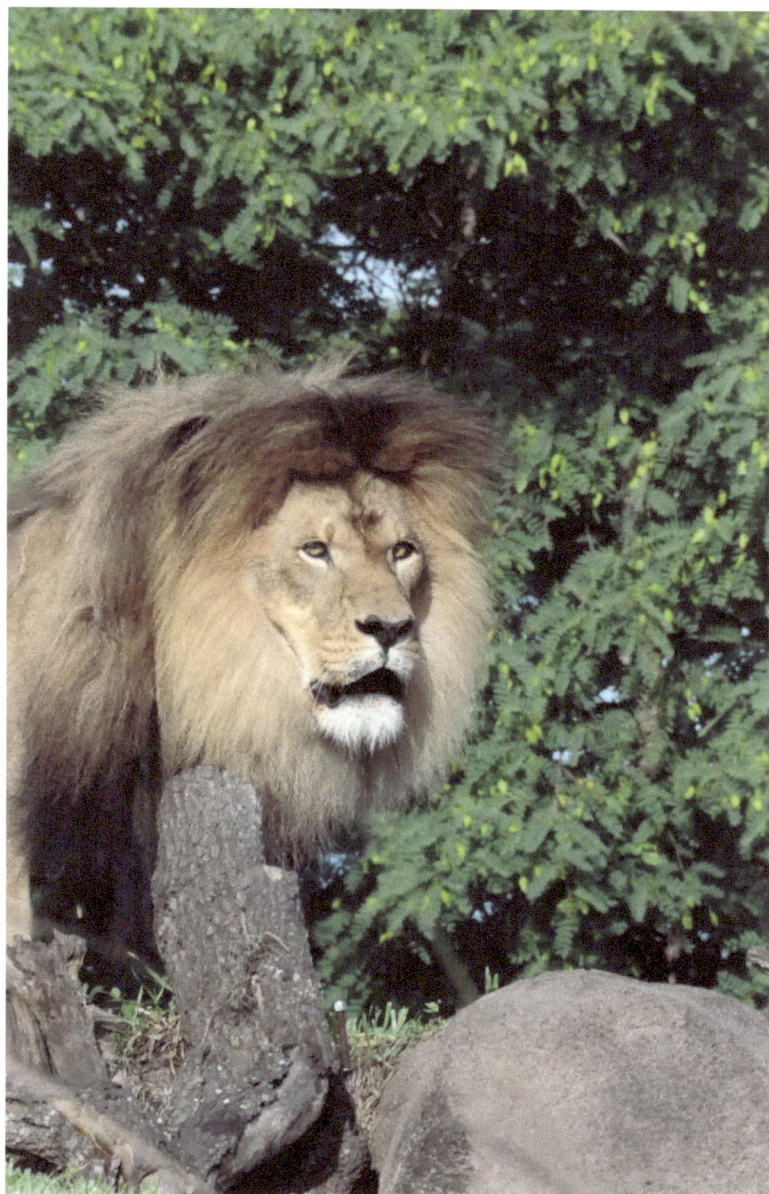

If ever an orangutan came down from the trees

Reasoning deforestation was just a tease

A challenge for a lumbering vast arm span

To use tools, gather, and carry out a plan

The solitary, reddish, and sobering face

Canopies through naked land in disgrace.

If ever the rhino traveled back in time

When in their evolutionary prime

Before archaic horns had priceless worth

Counting down 'til the last one on earth

Surveilled at gunpoint on the remaining's behalf

What tragic irony to world's worst gaffe.

If ever a tortoise emerges from ocean swell

With barnacle laden ancient hard shell

To bask and dry in sunlit glow

Then submerge sluggishly slow

Its dwelling a rugged simplistic life

Outliving elders despite its strife.

If ever a tiger growled so fierce

And flashed its teeth and claws to pierce

Stalking prey in vicious stranglehold

Brilliant orange and black stripes to behold

Downhill course from rampant poaching

Lack of habitat fast approaching.

If ever a panda wasn't so cute

When skillfully holding a bamboo chute

With fuzzy thick fur of white and black

Playfully frolicking on its back

Wandering carelessly all about

Preservation essential without a doubt.

If ever gazing amid the stars at night

Contemplating our creatures' fateful plight

Filtering the peaceful nocturnal sounds

As nightfall approaches and darkness surrounds

Witnessing nature's breathless beauty

Preserving pristine Earth our duty.

If ever animals could communicate what they understand

About the senseless destruction in waters and on land.

And how humans recklessly die and wage war with each other

Akin to species that vanish one after another.

Wondering how human beings survive
and are not extinct

Given that we are all so closely genetically
linked,

With profound differences in how we
battle a rival

Yet similarities in daily needs and the fight
for survival.

Human destruction measures like endangered beasts

If only deaths could be prevented or ceased.

The creatures would ponder and then make the case

Perhaps animals might outsmart the human race.

If ever the habitats of creatures were left untouched

Like a herd of wildebeest or hatchlings clutched

Ponder how Earthlings might have evolved

If the problems of the world were ever solved

The true meaning of what constitutes wild

Is diminishing the beguiled and exiled.

If ever bison could be an example

Of how to spread seeds through treacherous trample

Near threatened, lacking a diverse gene pool

Almost losing these beasts would have been cruel

Able to roam in conservation herds for grazing

Their comeback through Earthlings United nothing short of amazing.

If ever a polar bear walked in the snow

How mighty the arctic king would grow

With huge paws, black nose, and camouflage coat

Living in places barren and remote

Its appetite unceasing, hunting seals to survive

With numbered days will no longer thrive.

If ever elephants parade a dusty path

Their unassuming presence a mighty wrath

Baking in hot sun with weathered dark skin

Their elongated trunks cling newborn fragile kin

Yielding a magnificent trumpeting roar

These statuesque creatures may survive no more.

If ever all the Earthlings of the world unite

And saved endangered species from their plight

And returned to a time more pure

For only one thing we can assure

Our responsibility to all creatures great and small

Represents the most beastly task of all.

If ever the blue whale surfaced to exhale

It then submerges for krill in waters frail

This ultimate navigator of oceans

Is really nature's yacht in slow motion

Louder than a high-speed jet

Humans by far its greatest threat.

If ever a bumblebee knew its full power

Much more than humming flower to flower

A sting on occasion disturbs its buzz

Striped in black and yellowy fuzz

Essential for pollinating many a plant

Dwindling will leave the environment scant.

If ever a gorilla knew it was the greatest of apes

Swaying through marvelous tropical landscapes

Assembling in silverback families of dozens

With raw emotions akin to primal cousins

For if this powerful beast had no remaining jungle

Mankind's latest victim of our greatest bungle.

If ever the solitary koala could move faster

It may be more likely to survive natural disaster

And have more time to nap in trees

Or binge on eucalyptus eating sprees

This fuzzy marsupial's tranquil state

Inevitably needs help to alter its fate.

If ever a red panda climbed through the bamboo trees

With its bushy long tail sashaying in the breeze

Walking through the Himalayas with balance and grace

Cinnamon fur amid white whiskers on the sweetest kitten-like face

This animal family needs help to last

Or these beautiful Earthlings will be a creature of the past

If ever the zoo became ancient history

Leaving behind an unsolvable mystery

Creatures great and small now gone extinct

Inhabitable conditions a futile, inexplicable link.

A world not fit for beautiful beast

Precious wonders whom superiors ceased.

Whatever decimated animals on earth

Has left behind a desolate dearth.

In hope of uniting Earthlings everywhere.

www.ingramcontent.com/pod-product-compliance
Lightning Source LLC
Chambersburg PA
CBHW041442290326
41933CB00035B/214